WALKING TALKING WORDS

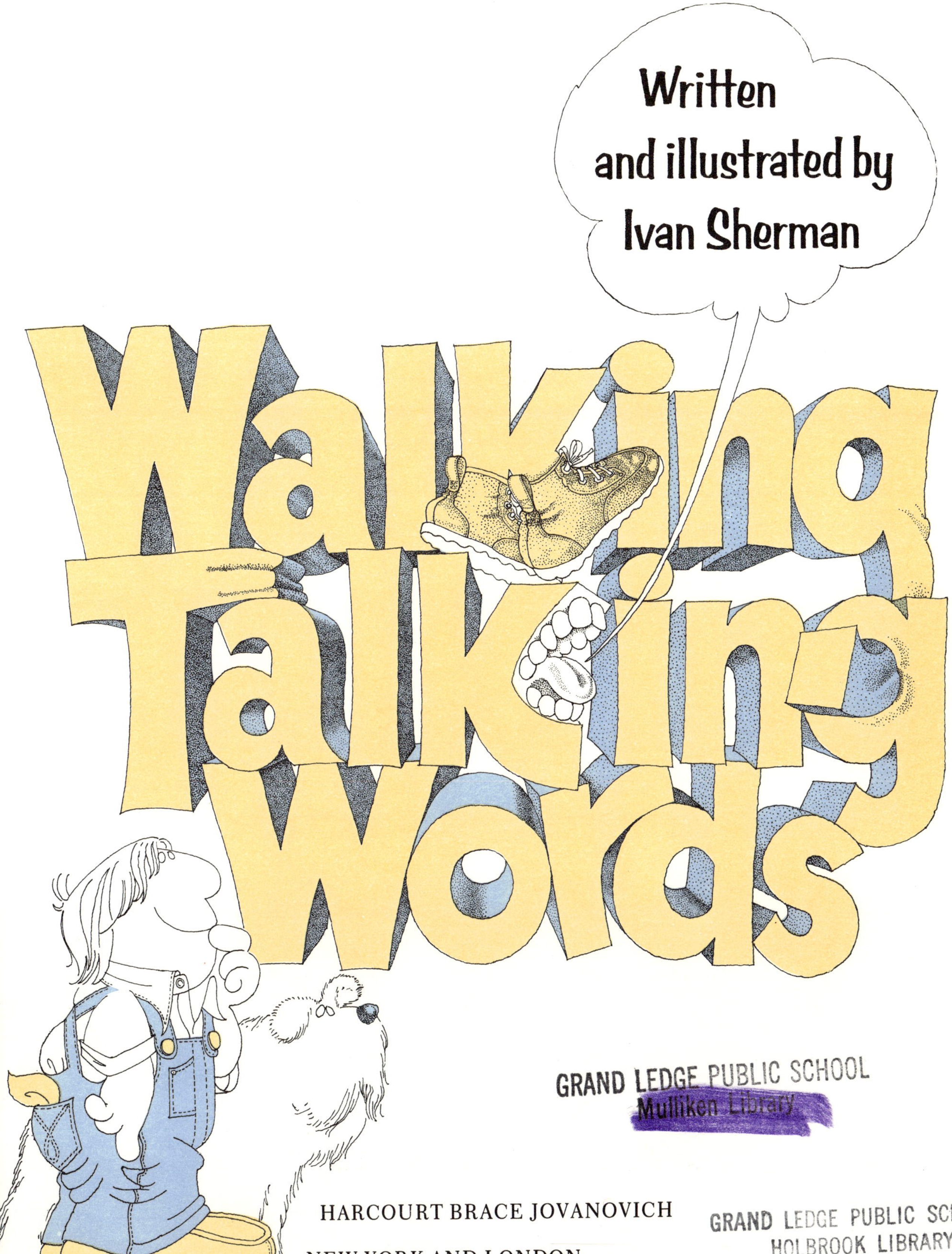

Walking Talking Words

Written and illustrated by Ivan Sherman

HARCOURT BRACE JOVANOVICH

NEW YORK AND LONDON

by the same author
Robert and the Magic String
I Do Not Like It When My Friend Comes to Visit
I Am a Giant

Copyright © 1980 by Ivan Sherman

All rights reserved. No part of this publication may be reproduced or transmitted in any form or by any means, electronic or mechanical, including photocopy, recording, or any information storage and retrieval system, without permission in writing from the publisher.

Requests for permission to make copies of any part of the work should be mailed to: Permissions, Harcourt Brace Jovanovich, Inc., 757 Third Avenue, New York, New York 10017

Printed in the United States of America

LIBRARY OF CONGRESS CATALOGING IN PUBLICATION DATA
Sherman, Ivan. Walking talking words.
SUMMARY: Limericks provide clues
for the simple words hidden within the accompanying illustrations.
1. Limericks—Juvenile literature.   2. Picture puzzles—Juvenile literature.
[1. Limericks.   2. Picture puzzles]   I. Title.
PN6231.L5S38   811'.54   80-13760
ISBN 0-15-294511-3

FIRST EDITION   B C D E

For the lady who
cherished all my pictures
and cheered all my words—
my mother, Bessie

Oh, little dog down at my feet,
They tell me that you're very sweet,
   But you nipped at my nose.
   Now you're nibbling my toes.
You must think I'm something to *eat*.

I really don't know how or why
I managed to get up so high,
And now I don't know
How to get back below.
Can anyone teach me to *fly*?

Remember how Mary Lou Fox
Covered a table with cream cheese and lox?
   Her mother said, "Please be neat, dear,
     If you want to eat here,
Or you'll eat all your meals in a *box*."

You better not make Lizzy cry.
Her big brother will want to know why.
　　He won't care if you're right.
　　He'll just start a fight,
And you'll get a punch in the *eye*.

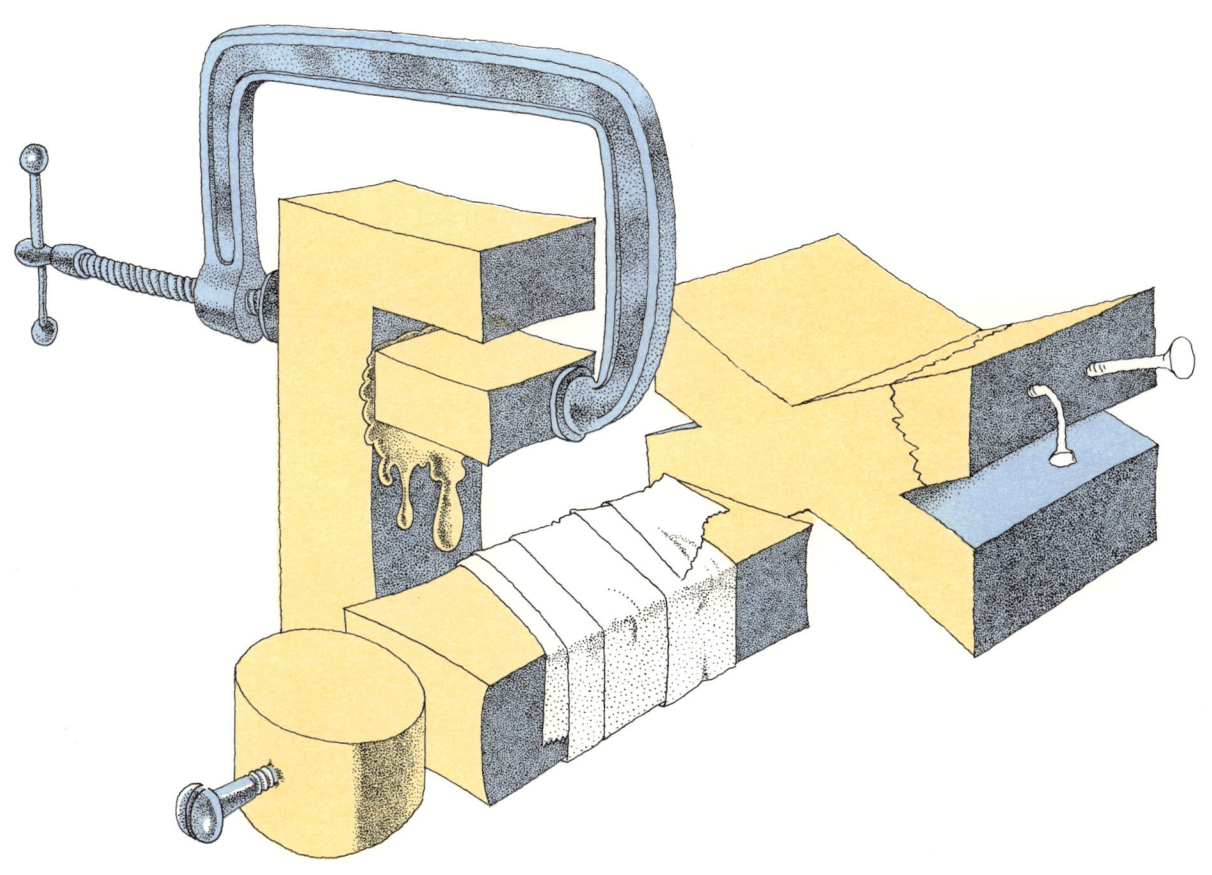

Willy loved to do tricks,
Like juggling bottles and bricks,
  Till his mother said, "You
    Better get nails and glue,
Because what you break, you will *fix.*"

I feel sorry for Jimmy Chopin.
His cereal bowl he put soap in.
   Now bubbles he blows.
   They rise out of his nose,
Or his mouth when he keeps it wide *open*.

She'll tickle your stomach like this,
Then she'll grab for your nose. She won't miss.
   She'll pinch at your cheek,
    And you'll giggle and shriek,
Until you give Mommy a *kiss*.

I have tangles all over my hair,
And there's nothing clean I can wear.
   There are knots in my shoe.
   My socks have holes too.
I'll just sit here and sulk in my *chair*.

When told she was getting too plump,
Polly answered, "Don't be a grump!
  I could be thinner,
    But I'd have to skip dinner.
Besides, now I bounce when I *jump*."

I once met a fellow named Salk,
Who insisted his dog was a hawk.
  He said, "Bye and bye
  I will teach him to fly.
But first he must learn how to *walk*."

There are papers all over the floor.
They are blowing right out of the drawer.
   There's dust in my eyes,
     And you're letting in flies.
Won't somebody please shut the *door*?

There's an artist I know who's the Law.
He's the sheriff, the marshal and more.
   He faced fifteen men,
    With just crayons and pen,
And beat them all to the *draw*.

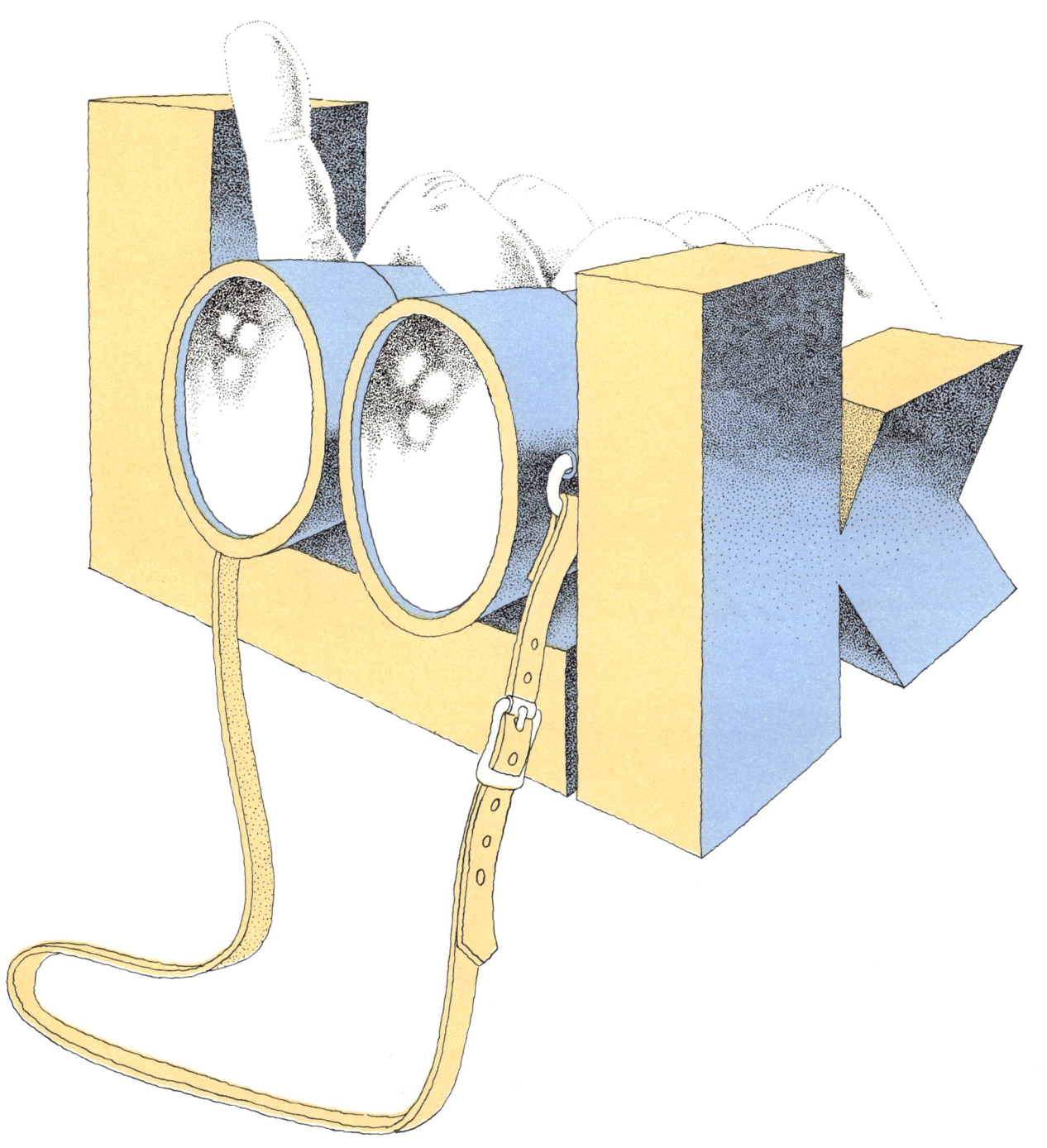

Has anyone here seen my book?
Was it borrowed, or lost, or just took?
   It's only a year
    Since I left it right here,
And now I don't know where to *look*.

I guess we could go for a walk,
Or cover a blackboard with chalk,
But I've so much to say
That maybe today
We'll just sit on the sofa and *talk*.

When going upstairs take your time.
That is the point of this rhyme.
   You'll just have to stop
   When you get to the top,
And then down again you will *climb*.

Sally's mother said she mustn't keep
All her clothes on the bed in a heap.
   Sally said, "But what for?
   I'll just empty a drawer
And climb into my dresser to *sleep*."

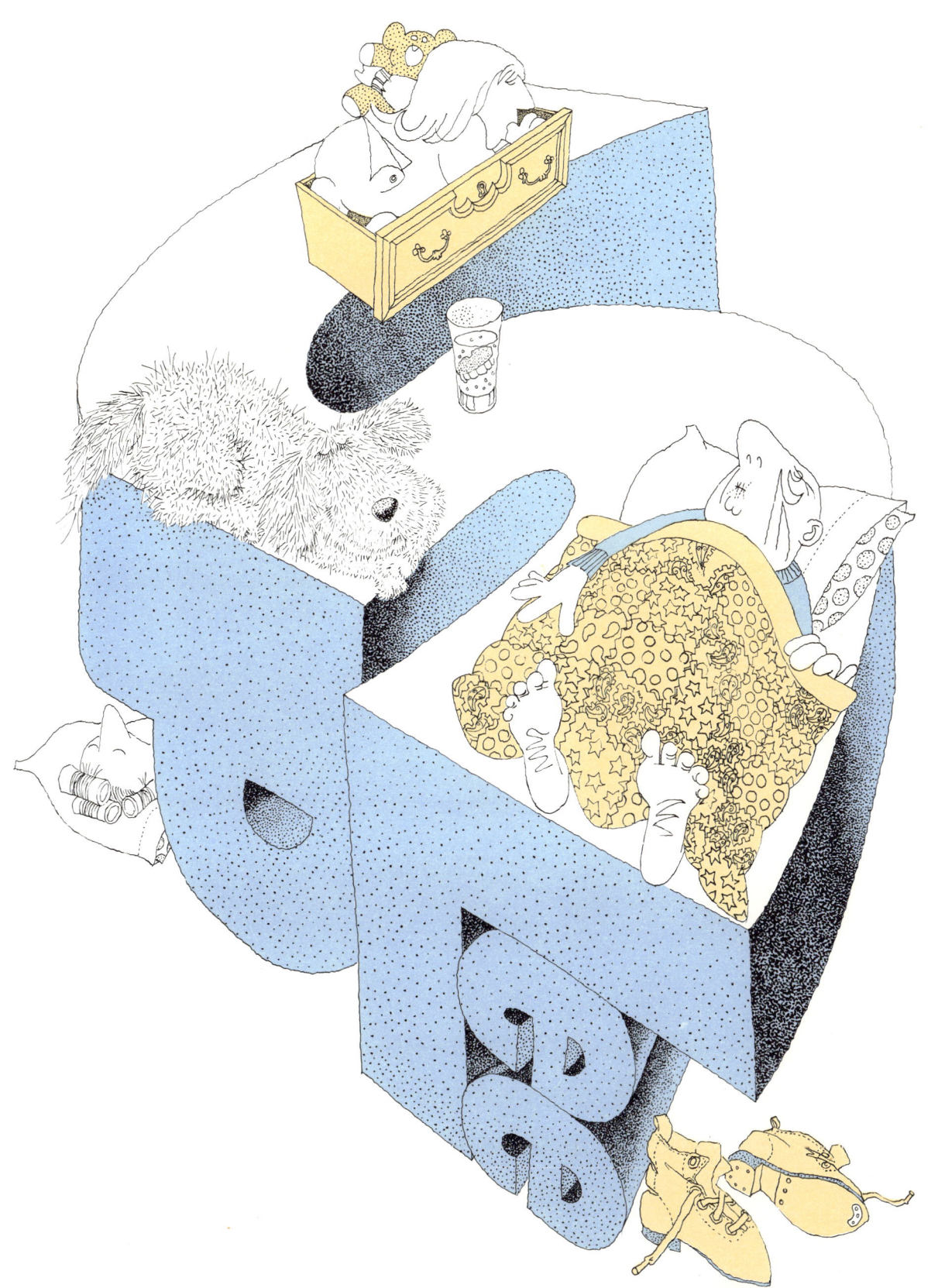

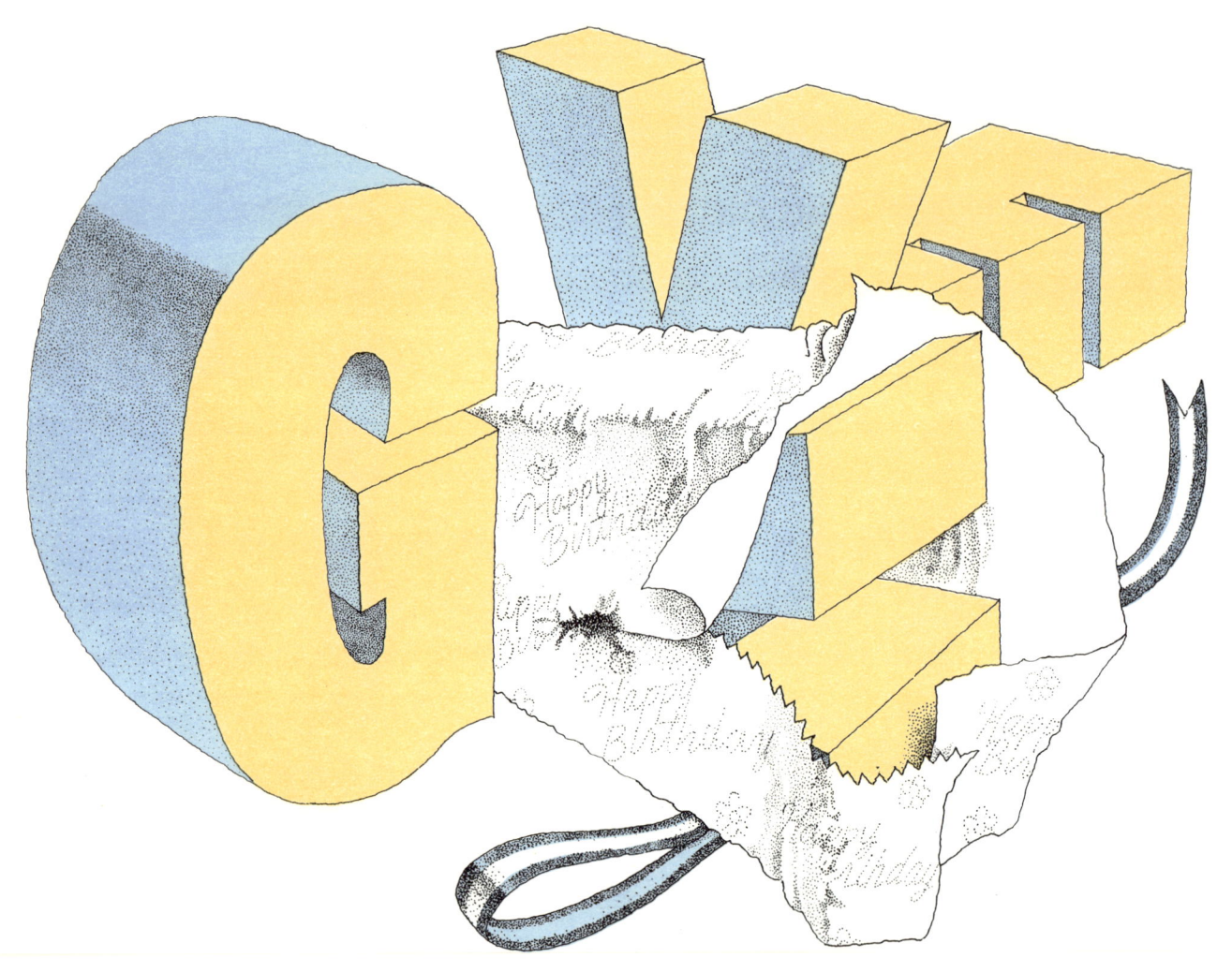

I hate buying presents for Dave!
I spend every cent I can save.
   I shop and I shop,
     Yet my gifts always flop,
Because he already has what I *gave*.

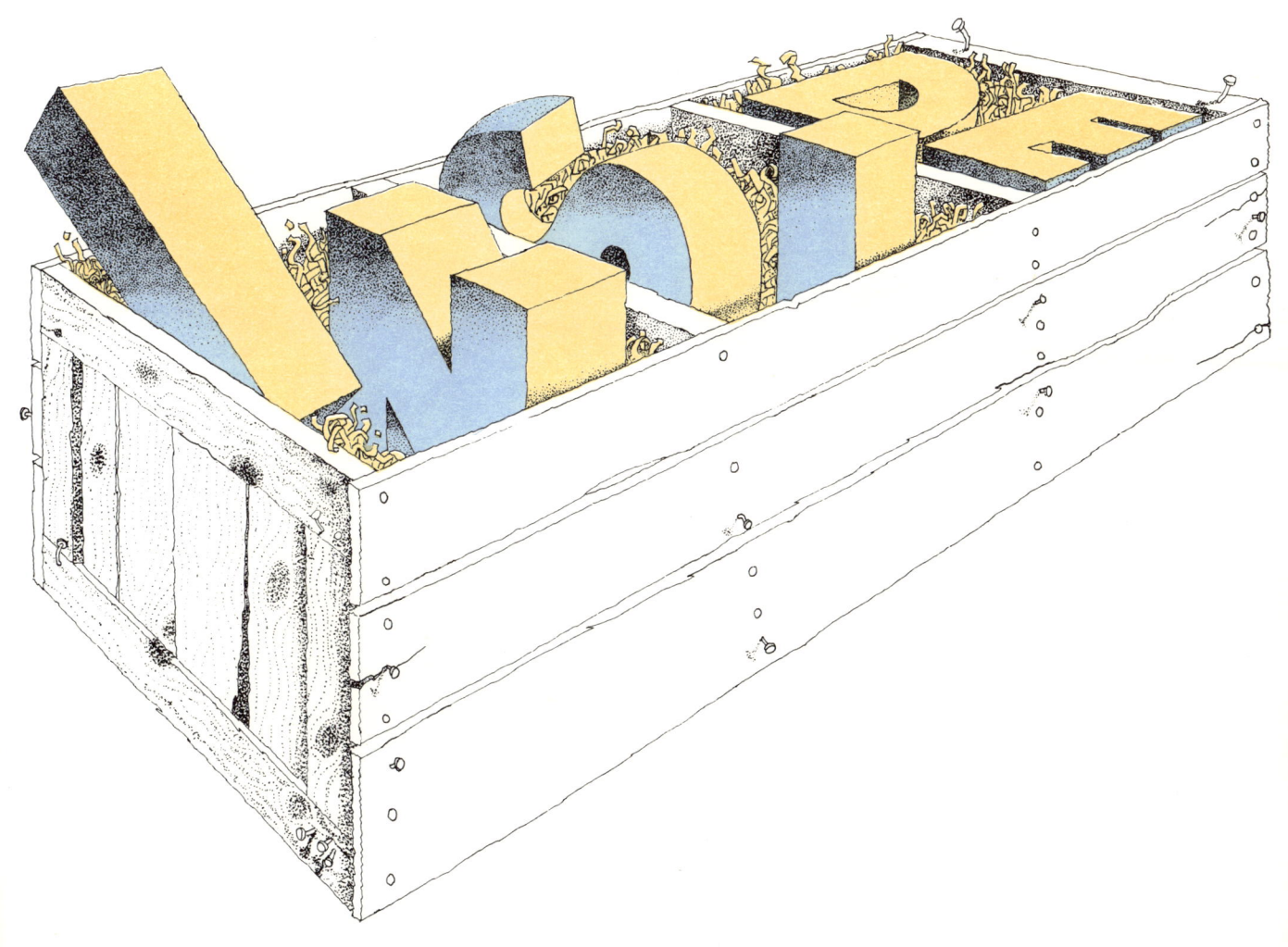

Oliver Oyster took pride,
"I'll never be baked, broiled, or fried,
 Because Mother did tell
 Me to stay in my shell
And never let strangers *inside*."

Some letters, you know, make a "bang!"
While other letters go "clang!"
  There are letters that "ring,"
    Some even "sing,"
But these can do nothing but *"hang."*

You always ought to say please
And never, ever tease.
   Take my advice,
   Always be nice,
Or you'll hang by your toes from the *trees*.

You'll love meeting Great Aunt Louise.
She always tries so hard to please.
   Just one thing may bug you;
   If she wants to hug you,
She might break your ribs with her *squeeze*.

I'm sorry but I have to go.
So long, good-bye, cheerio.
　I do have to leave . . .
　　So let go of my sleeve,
And stop shaking my hand "*Hello*."

811　　　Sherman, Ivan
Sh
　　　　Walking, talking
　　　words

DATE DUE

NO 11 '81			
JA 4 '82			
MY 3 '82			
MY 21 '82			
AP 29 '85			
MY 21 '87			
OC 17 '88			

DEMCO